Xmas 1991

To Hamish
with fond love
from
Alistair, Anne
Jamie, Kirsten & Fiona

# THE SEVEN SHAIKHDOMS

Ruler's fort at Abu Dhabi in 1949. The old fort was enclosed by a new wall added in the mid 1930s. The shelter for the guards can be seen behind the main entrance.

# THE SEVEN SHAIKHDOMS

## Life in the Trucial States before the federation of the United Arab Emirates

### RONALD CODRAI

*To Bamela*

**Editor**
Anthony Lejeune

**Designer**
Keith Savage

The Seven Shaikhdoms

First Published in 1990 by
Stacey International
128 Kensington Church Street
London W8 4BH
Telex 298768 Stacey G
Fax 071 792 9288

© Ronald Codrai and Stacey International 1990

Set in Linotype Plantin
by SX Composing Ltd, Rayleigh, Essex
Printed & Bound in Singapore
by Times Publishing Group

British Library Cataloguing in Publication Data
Codrai Ronald
Seven shaikhdoms: life in the Trucial States before the
federation of the United Arab Emirates

1. United Arab Emirates, history
I. Title
953'.57
ISBN 0-905743-58-X

ISBN 0 905743 58 X

**Previous page** *Barasti* (palm frond) dwellings clustered on the creekside of
Dubai, with Shandaga in the background. An in-flow of water separated
the two parts of the town at high tide. **Below** Crossing the *Maqta'a* – the
ford separating Abu Dhabi island from the mainland – at low tide. The
watchtower in the centre of the ford was constantly manned by armed
guards from Abu Dhabi.

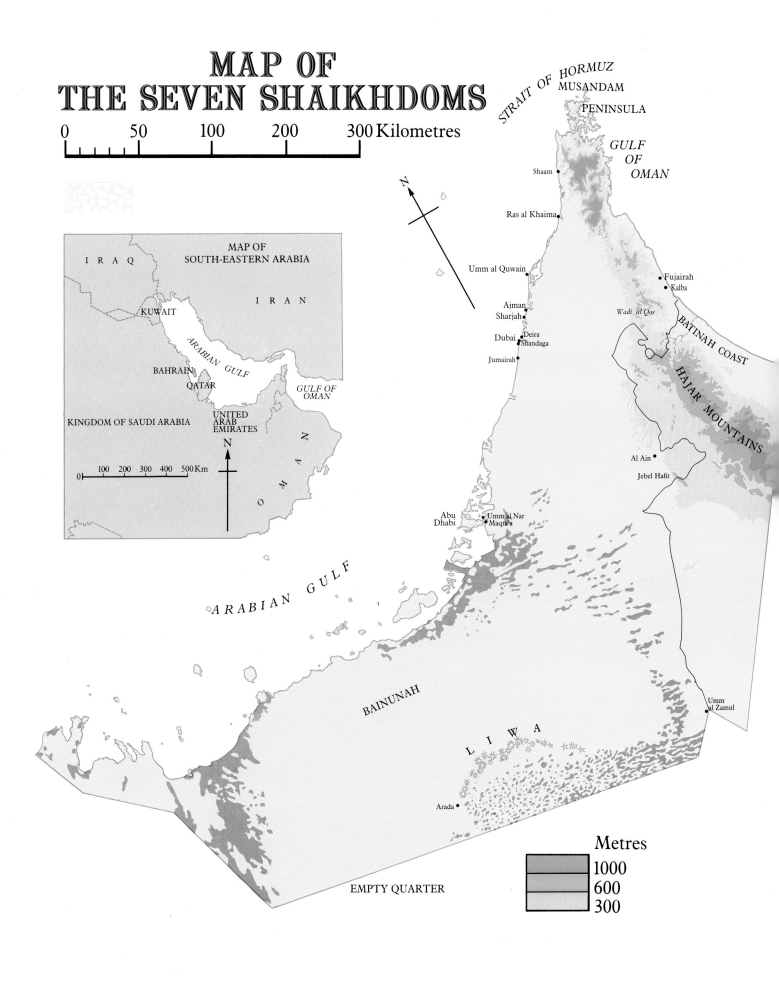

# MAP OF
# THE SEVEN SHAIKHDOMS

0    50    100    200    300 Kilometres

MAP OF
SOUTH-EASTERN ARABIA

I R A Q

I R A N

KUWAIT

*ARABIAN GULF*

BAHRAIN
QATAR

*GULF OF
OMAN*

KINGDOM OF SAUDI ARABIA

UNITED
ARAB
EMIRATES

O
M
A
N

N

0    100  200  300  400  500 Km

N

*STRAIT OF HORMUZ*
MUSANDAM
PENINSULA

*GULF
OF
OMAN*

Shaam

Ras al Khaima

Umm al Quwain

Fujairah
Kalba

Ajman
Sharjah

*Wadi al Qor*

BATINAH COAST

Dubai Deira
Shandaga

Jumairah

*HAJAR MOUNTAINS*

Al Ain

Jebel Hafit

Abu
Dhabi

Umm al Nar
Maqta'a

*ARABIAN GULF*

BAINUNAH

Umm
al Zamul

L I W A

Arada

EMPTY QUARTER

Metres

1000
600
300

# CONTENTS

Sharjah roof tops. A view of Sharjah from the south in 1950 with the sea in the background. Different styles of windtowers can be seen including, on the left, the only round windtower in the area.

# INTRODUCTION

IN 1948 I went to live in the corner of Arabia now known as the United Arab Emirates. At that time it was not a single state but a group of seven Shaikhdoms, which had much in common with each other but maintained their independence.

Shortly after my first visit I joined an international oil consortium whose concessions blanketed many countries of the Arab world, including all the coastal

territories from Qatar to Aden. (Had it not been for a dispute about whether the annual rent should be thirty thousand pounds sterling or thirty thousand pounds gold, the consortium would also have owned the oil concession for Saudi Arabia.) Not being a technician, I was sent to an 'outpost' where my liaison work with the Rulers who had granted the as yet unworked oil concessions, gave me ample opportunity to travel throughout the Shaikhdoms and into neighbouring Oman.

It was often a lonely existence and I derived great satisfaction from my lifelong hobby of photography. With camera and notebook I recorded much of what I saw, not for posterity but for my own pleasure. During my thirty-five years in some fifteen Arab countries, I have amassed a large number of photographs, but those I took in the Shaikhdoms reveal the most dramatic changes.

I've become increasingly aware of the speed at which photographs can become of historical interest. Suddenly, it seems to me, the pictures I took a mere forty years ago now constitute the only record of a way of life that has gone. Since their vocabulary had no word for cameras, the people of the Shaikhdoms imaginatively referred to them as *aks* – reflections. Few of those who good naturedly posed for me, or accompanied me on my travels, have survived the passing of years, and it will be their offspring who view these pages, these reflections of yesterday.

Shaikh Zaid bin Sultan, the first President of the United Arab Emirates, recalling to a university audience the privation, drought, poverty and sometimes hunger suffered by people of the Shaikhdoms in earlier times, urged his young listeners to learn from the fortitude and patience of their forefathers who survived such adversity. He concluded: 'I believe that he who does not know his past will not understand the present, nor will he be able to prepare himself for the future.'

I owe much to the Shaikhs and people of the Shaikhdoms for their friendship, kindness and humour. Peace be on them and their kin.

**Above** Ronald Codrai receives Shaikh Mohammed bin Salim (left) of Ras al Khaima (father of Shaikh Saqr the present ruler), and his son Shaikh Humaid (right). **Right** Deira. The ferry boat (*abra*) landing stage at the *suq* in Deira.

8

# LOOKING BACK

THE SHAIKHDOMS were Abu Dhabi (Father of a Gazelle), Dubai, Sharjah, Ajman, Umm al Quwain, Ras al Khaima (Point of the Tent) and Fujairah. Outside the region they were known collectively by various descriptive names: Trucial Shaikhdoms, Trucial Coast, Trucial Oman, Pirate Coast, Coast of Oman and later, Trucial States; the word 'Trucial' being derived from nineteenth century treaties between each of the Shaikhdoms and Great Britain. In 1971, nine years after their oil was first exported, these territories entered into a Federation which they called the United Arab Emirates.

I lived in the Shaikhdoms for eight years, at a time when they were little known outside the region, even in other parts of the Arab world. Although on the brink of change, their distinctive traditional way of life had scarcely been disturbed. There were no boundaries and no roads, no newspapers and no telephones, indeed no electricity supply. Almost every drop of water had to be hauled from man-dug wells. Transistors had not arrived; only a few urban dwellers, able to charge a car battery possessed radios. The only form of police or security force was the retinue of armed tribesmen maintained by each of the Shaikhs. There was no need of clocks; the only divisions of the day which mattered were the times for prayer, and these were determined by the position of the sun. In the more remote areas, it was as though the wheel had not been invented.

Outside the little towns and villages, one rarely met a man not armed with a dagger and rifle and bandolier of ammunition. Even in town, men of tribal origin felt insecure without their weapons, for raids and abductions were commonplace.

Before the search for oil began, no-one cared about formal frontiers. What counted were the spheres of influence of the leading Shaikhs, and tribal areas based on water and grazing rights, but even they were ill-defined and frequently overlapping. An armed escort was essential if one travelled inland. Except for the nomadic tribesmen, travel was chiefly by sea, to other Gulf ports or to Bombay. As well as the many sailing craft plying the Gulf, a British India Line steamer carrying passengers, mail and some cargo, made round trips from Bombay, one up the Gulf and one down every two weeks. The ships anchored out at sea, lighters bobbing around them. In Sharjah, a small RAF Staging Post was kept supplied by a weekly Dakota flight from Habaniyah in Iraq. Until the late 1940s a mere handful of people from all the States of the Gulf had ever been to Europe. Trade routes to Iran, India and East Africa were easier than those to the main capitals of the Arab world and the far-flung Ottoman Empire never extended as far as the Shaikhdoms, mainly due to British political effort.

**Previous page** Khalifa's Tower on the Khabaiba side of Shandaga. **Above** Entrance to Abu Dhabi fort.

Dotted along the western shore were small ports and villages, most of them situated beside salt-water inlets with drinking water available from nearby wells. Beyond the coastal stretches of *sabkha* – salt-flats-cum-gypsum marshes – lay the desert, sand gradually building up until the dunes were six hundred feet high. They were the start of the greatest sand mass on our planet, the Empty Quarter desert covering the greater part of southern Arabia. To the east it was bounded by gravel plains under the Hajar mountains. The further the mountains stood back from the sea, the more desolate became the coastline. The only inhabited place between Dubai, the Shaikhdoms' largest port and trading centre, and Qatar was Abu Dhabi. Situated on an island linked to the mainland by a tidal ford, it consisted of little more than one large fort, a few (mostly crumbling) houses built of coral stone and a hundred or so huts made from palm fronds. In great contrast, beyond the Hajar mountains, on the Gulf of Oman, a fertile strip of land extended north to the Shaikhdom of Fujairah and south as far as Muscat.

Fishing, the rearing of camels and goats and the cultivation of the date palm constituted virtually the only indigenous sources of food. Pearling and maritime trades provided the means to buy whatever had to be imported, notably such basic foodstuffs as rice, flour, sugar, coffee and ghee (clarified butter). Although entirely Arab and Islamic, the

some minimal way by bedu in a remote area. A clean shirt or headcloth might not be available, but the beard could be trimmed, the head shaved, or the eyes lined with kohl, acknowledging that the day was special.

Change, when it finally came was at a breathtaking pace. During the quarter of a century following the discovery of oil the Shaikhdoms have altered beyond all recognition. Small settlements have grown into large modern towns. Agricultural projects have been launched. There has been much greening of the desert and landscaping of towns and highways. Here and there, sand dunes have been levelled and the coastline reshaped by land reclamation. New international airports could handle the entire population several times a year.

Abu Dhabi in 1949. The Ruler's fort can be seen to the right of the town.

Abu Dhabi in 1959. The British political agent's residency lies between the fort and the shore.

Shaikhdoms took a little of their special character from the places with which they traded in India, Iran and Africa.

Religious faith was absolute, giving its followers a code for daily living as well as spiritual comfort. Lacking material help and comforts, people tended to be fatalistic. No reference could be made to the future without the reservation 'If God wills' (*Insha'Allah*). God, and not the host, was thanked for food. Prayers, one of the five pillars of Islam, were said five times a day, and Friday (which, like the other days of the week, began at sunset on the preceeding day) was always observed as the 'Day of Assembly', the Muslim Sabbath, even if only in

The briefcase has replaced the gun, the motor car has usurped the camel. Air-conditioning has become so ubiquitous, in homes, cars, offices and hotels that the climate itself might have been transformed – a far cry from the days when the greatest luxury was a windtower gently wafting humid air on to the people beneath it, leaving their backs soaked in perspiration.

Today's museums are filled with exhibits which were in everyday use only a few years ago. Once prominent forts and watchtowers are dwarfed or lost in the high-rise developments around them. They have become the cherished symbols of a bygone time.

**Left** Fujairah. Taken from the mountains to the north-west of the town. **Top** Ruler's fort Fujairah built on a mound and surrounded by houses. **Above** A watchtower guards the approaches to Fujairah from the north.

**Above left** Ras al Khaima. Looking towards the creek from the top of the Ruler's fort. **Above** Small fortress belonging to the Ruler of Abu Dhabi in the vicinity of Al Ain.
**Top** Sharjah airstrip – now the middle of downtown Sharjah – laid out over *sabkha*, and the main staging post in the area.
**Left** Jebel Hafit: a prominent landmark on the main route south across the plain into central Oman.

**Top left** Umm al Quwain taken from over the sea. The largest rectangular building in the centre was the Ruler's fort. **Left** Ruler's fort at Ajman with the town behind it. The sea is beyond. **Above** A locust swarm crosses the coast at Dubai, with Deira in the background.

**Left** The creek between Shandaga and Dubai overflowed at high tide. **Top** Sailmakers of Shandaga work on a lateen sail staked out on the sands at Khabaiba. **Above** The three communities of Dubai's creek – Dubai proper on the right, Deira across the creek, and Shandaga straggling along the sea. **Following pages** The Ruler's fort Sharjah.

# PORTRAIT GALLERY

DID SOMEBODY-THE-GREAT really look as fearsome as historical records suggest? What did Falan bin Falan, who begat so many children, look like? Photographs, though they may not be entirely accurate portrayals of character, do provide some visual basis for our knowledge of the past. Unfortunately, the people of the Shaikhdoms were comparatively late in starting their family albums. The only exceptions were the few who visited the portrait studios of Bombay or similar ports of call where photography was already in vogue.

The portrait photographs which I took during my stay in the Shaikhdoms were not designed for posterity. My subjects were simply people I knew and liked. It says much for their open mindedness that the camera, an unfamiliar object, was never taboo: the results tended to amuse them.

In general, I prefer spontaneous photographs as posed portraits seem less natural and lack context. Lighting was always a problem. The sun overhead cast deep shadows under headcloths and into the eyes. I tried to overcome this by reflecting light into the shadows from a piece of card on which I had stuck the silver paper from many cigarette tins, but it looked artificial. Much better, if time allowed, was to wait until the sun was low, providing a softer, more even light over the whole face. When we were within reach of an electrical supply, bulbs mounted in aluminium cooking pots gave me greater control, but it still seemed unnatural to photograph my subjects against a piece of cloth, when they should have been seen against a background of sky, sea or desert. However, the interest of the subject exceeds any merit the photographs may have.

Viewing my portraits of Rulers, Shaikhs, bedu, seafarers and merchants, I see people of great character, a fine breed whose countenances radiate something of their spiritual attitude. Their faces portray the hardship of their lives; the determined expression of people who accepted life's challenge with great fortitude, feeling themselves in direct communion with a God to whom they entrusted their destinies. These are also the faces of people who are not slow to smile and had the self-assurance of their own aristocracy.

H.H. Shaikh Zayed bin Sultan al Nahayyan, born 1918. First
President of the United Arab Emirates from 1971 and Ruler
of Abu Dhabi since 1966, photographed by the author in
mid-century like the others in this chapter.

Shaikh Shakbut bin Sultan bin Zayed (1903-1989), Ruler of
Abu Dhabi from 1928 to 1966.

Shaikh Said bin Maktoum al Juma (1878-1958), Ruler of
Dubai from 1912 to 1958.

H.H. Shaikh Rashid bin Said al Maktoum (born 1912), first Vice-President of the United Arab Emirates since 1971 and Ruler of Dubai from 1958.

**Top** Third from the left, the late Shaikh Mohammed bin Saqr al Qasimi, acting Ruler of Sharjah in 1951 and father of the present Ruler of Sharjah. Next to him in the centre, Shaikh Saqr bin Sultan al Qasimi, Ruler of Sharjah from 1951-1965. **Above** Shaikh Mohammed bin Hamad al Sharqi (1908-1975), first Ruler of Independent Fujairah 1952-1975, stands before a group of his subjects and retainers.

Shaikh Ahmed bin Rashid al Mualla (1908-1981), Ruler of
Umm al Quwain from 1929 to 1981.

Centre of the three nearest the camera Shaikh Rashid bin Humaid al Nuaimi
(1904-1981) Ruler of Ajman from 1928 to 1981. On his right is his son Shaikh
Ali and on his left his son, Shaikh Humaid, present Ruler of Ajman.

H.H. Saqr bin Mohammed al Qawasimi (born 1920), Ruler
of Ras al Khaima from 1948.

Shaikh Mohammed bin Hamad al Sharqi (1908-1975), first ruler of Fujairah,
with retainers.

**Top** Shaikh Hamad bin Said, Ruler of Kalba from 1937-1951.
The man on his right is his brother Shaikh Salim. **Above**
Shaikh Khalid bin Ahmed, Ruler of Sharjah from 1914-1924
and Regent of Kalba from 1937-1943.

H.H. Shaikh Hamad bin Mohammed al Sharqi, Ruler of Fujairah since 1975, photographed with his protectors. His father was Shaikh Mohammed bin Hamad al Sharqi, Ruler of Fujairah from 1952 to 1975.

# MERCHANT MARINERS

MANY DWELLERS in the Shaikhdoms were seafarers or otherwise connected with the sea; even the bedu often did seasonal work as fishermen or pearl divers. The Gulf has always been a trade route. In earliest times, copper for the bronze age world was mined in Oman, and by the tenth century locally built ships were trading the oceans from Africa to China, carrying dates and pearls, and returning with cargoes of silk, frankincense, spices, ivory, timber, nuts and cloves, some of which were then carried from the head of the Gulf by caravan to Europe.

Although much of this trade had vanished long before my time, the ancient boat building tradition survived. Of greatest antiquity was a small, canoe-like craft, called a *shasha*, made from the stems of palm fronds tied together with palm fibres and soaked in fish oil for waterproofing. This method was still being used in the 1950s, but one saw few of the bigger vessels built by stitching together the timbers with a giant needle and cord. There were several designs evolved over the centuries which the West called, collectively, dhows. The essential features were a lateen rig (a triangular sail set at forty-five degrees to the mast) and a shallow hull. The grandest and most impressive was the *baghala*, with its galleon-like, windowed stern; it had a crew of more than twenty and could carry a cargo of five hundred tons. In the 1940s, however, it had been largely replaced by the *boom* which was more manoeuvrable and faster. The smaller *sambuq* was a good all-rounder for pearling and fishing and, without its deck, was used as a lighter. Another small and versatile craft was the *jelbut*, which later, when fitted with a diesel engine, became known in Arabic as 'launch'.

The shipwright's skill had been handed down through generations. He had no drawings to guide him; the plans were in his head. Boats were built anywhere along the populated parts of the coast where there was a suitable sandy beach. The length of the boat was determined by the length of the longest tree trunk available;

it went against the shipwright's instincts to make a keel by joining two lengths of timber. Then he shaped and arranged the ribs, fastening planks together with a trenail – a pin of hard wood – and caulked the seams with raw cotton or rope soaked in oil. The mainmast, which might rise ninety feet above the sea, was shaped from a single trunk. Large craft usually had a raised poopdeck. Finally, the outside of the hull was coated with a boiled mixture of whitewash and grease, and the remainder of the vessel with shark's oil to prevent warping. These coatings were renewed once or twice a year and on a humid day the stench of shark oil hung over the port.

Launching, whether of a new craft or of a boat that had been beached for cleaning, was a boisterous affair. To the accompaniment of chanting and the beat of a drum the boat was heaved towards the water until a great cheer proclaimed her afloat.

At each port of call the *nakhuda* (the captain, who might himself be a merchant) had to decide whether to carry another merchant's goods for a fixed price, or to buy goods himself. Often his cargo would be a mixture of the two, and might include some fare-paying passengers as well. If the voyage was to Zanzibar, Mombasa or one of the other East African ports, he might buy a return cargo of *chandals* (mangrove poles, used for building and making *barasti* houses) for which there was usually a good market in the Shaikhdoms or even take his vessel into the mosquito swamps and have his crew cut the poles, a very unpopular task.

As the stars faded each morning the *nakhuda* would descend from his bed on the navigator's bench, high across the stern, to perform the dawn prayers. Breakfast consisted of sweet tea without milk, unleavened bread and, as a luxury, vermicelli with sugar or honey, followed by bitter coffee. During the morning the decks were washed, and repairs made. An almost endless task was the plaiting and mending of cables made from coconut fibre. On a long voyage the ship's carpenter might build a small boat to sell at one of the ports of call. Other sailors would make model boats for sale, or hammer elaborate patterns of brass studs into heavy wooden chests, or re-bottle perfumes ready for sale.

Cooking was done on a wood or charcoal fire in an enclosed fire-box. Fresh water was carried in large, wooden, skin-lined tanks. Sometimes the crew had to endure brackish or foul water, either because there had been nothing else at their last port of call, or because some vendor had cheated them by drawing water from the poorest wells.

Entering port was a showy business. The ship might be towed by a long boat full of rowing, chanting sailors, or the *nakhuda* might bring her in at speed, under sail, turning into the wind at the last moment. To stop her, sailors often had to dive overboard and attach lines to other boats. As the vessel arrived at a strange village or town, the crew gathered in the bows and, with their hands cupped, chorused loudly and slowly the greeting '*salaam alaikum*'.

When in port, carpets were placed on the poop, surrounded with cushions and the sailors' decorated chests, and an awning was erected overhead. The sailors groomed themselves for visits ashore or to other vessels. Fresh meat and delicacies were carried aboard. Under the light of a hurricane lamp the sound of voices, and sometimes of music and chanting, could be heard in the night long after the rest of the port had lapsed into silence and sleep.

**Page 36 and 37** In the 1940s many traditional craft which today are motorised were powered by sail. **Above** The lateen rig, highly effective when running before the wind, was otherwise cumbersome and had to be manhandled into position.

After several months on a voyage to Southern Arabia and East Africa, the *nakhuda* and crew of this *kutaiyah*, were anxious to know the price of mangrove poles. They wanted to estimate the value of their cargo and the profit they might have made.

**Above** The sailmaker only needed a flat stretch of ground on which to lay out his strips of canvas, and shape and sew them into a sail. Behind him stands a wooden water tank from a sailing ship.

Shipwrights acquired their skill through long apprenticeship. Boats were built on the beach above the high-water mark, for ease of launching. They used a few simple, but time-tested tools, the bow drill **below far left**, saw and plane. The adze **below left** is being used to fashion a mast from a single tree trunk which might be over ninety feet in length. **Right** Steering with the leg relieved the helmsman's arms on a long voyage. **Below** The *nakhuda* of the boat helps his crewmen to haul in the sail.

**Above** This mariner had voyaged under sail between the Gulf and East Africa to India.
**Left** This helmsman's *jelbut* was called 'El Ghannas'; the Hunter.

**Above** The *nakhuda* sleeps on his platform above the poop. A porous pot for keeping water cool hangs from a beam. **Right** A sailor ties up the sail.

**Left** Wooden hulls required constant maintenance. Careening, caulking, oiling with fish oil, and the application of an additional mixture of grease and whitewash below the waterline. **Top and above** In tidal waters any sandy shore might be used for beaching craft for repairs and maintenance.

One night in February 1950 a strong *shammal* swept the coast bringing winds of over 80 knots, causing the loss of some sixty boats and many lives. **Top** This boat came to grief trying to run for shelter into Dubai creek. It broke up and its cargo was lost. **Above** This *jelbut* was wrecked on the shore at Jumairah with the loss of eleven lives and all its cargo. Next morning the *nakhuda* **right** climbed up on to the boat's twisted poop to survey the damage.

GEM THAT
DIMS THE MOON

TOWARDS the end of May, the waterfronts of the little ports along the western shore of the Shaikhdoms hummed with activity as vessels were prepared for the pearling season. This scene had been re-enacted for countless years, but by the late 1940s the thousands of boats which used to be engaged in the Gulf's most important industry had dwindled to relatively few. The decline started in the 1930s with Japan's development of 'cultured' pearls and was accentuated by recession and changes of fashion in the West. Although the market for the more expensive natural pearls never really recovered after the Second World War, 'the dive' remained an important feature of life in the Shaikhdoms until the 1950s.

The traditional method of diving, virtually unchanged through the centuries, was simple but physically demanding. After the boat had been anchored off one of the innumerable pearling banks, the divers would slip into the water, and after a short period of noisy deep breathing, each would descend on a stone fastened to a rope paid out by the haulers. He had a wooden or bone clip over his nostrils, and, where the oysters were attached to coral, leather finger stalls to protect his fingers. Some of the oysters had to be prised off with a knife. The catch was placed in a string bag tied to the hauling line; when it was full, or the diver had reached his limit for staying submerged, he would jerk the line and be pulled swiftly to the surface by his hauler. He then rested in the water for a short while, holding on to a rope draped from an overhanging oar, while the oysters were added to the pile on deck.

Each man went on diving for up to an hour before taking a rest in the boat. At between sixty and a hundred dives a day, he must actually have been under water for a total of two to three hours: but no one counted. Although the amount of time a diver could stay under water was dramatically reduced by depth, I was told that a good diver could stay down for over two minutes even in very deep water. Some oyster banks were in quite shallow waters, others between twenty and fifty feet down. A few were very much deeper – maybe a hundred feet – and there was a general belief that the best pearls were to be found at these greater depths. A diver might collect twenty oysters at a time, but all too frequently he returned empty handed. The luckiest haul was a *tabarah*, a cluster of oysters which were stuck together, nearly always pearl bearing, and potentially highly profitable. Exceptionally, a single pearl of great size and beauty – such as Emerson had in mind when he called it 'the gem that dims the moon' – might represent a good profit for the whole season.

Casualties occurred every year. The divers shared the sea with sharks, barracuda and swordfish. Jelly-fish could inflict a painful sting which caused a fever lasting several days; when there were shoals of them about, divers wore one-piece cotton garments for protection. They sometimes claimed to have seen weird spectacles in the silent depths – headless camels, women armed with cutlasses, multi-headed monsters. Such hallucinations were attributed to evil *djinn*. If the diver had the 'bends' and was temporarily deranged by being hauled up too quickly, or if he suffered excruciating ear pains, he was covered with a sail and sat upon, religious verse read over him and frankincense burned under under his nostrils. As a last resort, he might be cauterised.

The oysters were opened on board in the evening or early in the morning, and every pearl found was passed to the *nakhuda*. They varied greatly in size, shape and colour. Many oysters were empty, but some contained numerous tiny seed pearls. A few of the largest shells were kept for sale to merchants dealing in mother-of-pearl, such as one of my neighbours in Dubai who shipped them to Germany where they were used mainly for making buttons.

Towards the end of September the boats came home. Loudly chanting, the crews rowed into port, drawing attention to themselves by splashing as well as pulling on their oars. Children clambered aboard to welcome back their fathers. It was a happy occasion, best if the pearling had been good, marred by financial worries if it had been a poor season.

The financial arrangement between the crew, the *nakhuda* and the merchants who financed the operation was well established. At the beginning of the season the merchant bought all the supplies for the trip and made cash advances to the crew with which to support their families. At the end of the season, when the pearls had been sold, the merchant would keep half the proceeds. From the other half he deducted the cost of the supplies before dividing the balance among the crew. Each man, from the *nakhuda* down to the cook's helper, received a set share according to his function, from which their personal cash advances had to be deducted. After a bad season members of the crew could find themselves in debt.

These debts, plus further cash advances to tide them over the winter, were carried forward into the next season's account.

One day, passing through the *suq*, I saw several pearl merchants squatting before a man who was working on something held between his finger and thumb. It proved to be a large but badly-shaped and faulty pearl, which he was 'skinning' with a small knife, while the merchants made their bids. Layer by layer its nacre was removed, like the skins of an onion. As its shape improved, higher bids were made for it. The owner had to decide each time whether to proceed further; removing one skin too many could greatly reduce its value.

The pearls were sorted and graded and traded perhaps many times, as they made their way to the world's markets via Bombay.

**Page 50 and 51** The crew of a pearling boat returning from a season's diving with their baskets and ropes on which the divers descended. **Above** Unsorted pearls purchased by a merchant directly from the boats at the pearling banks.

**Right** With months of hardship and privation behind them, pearlers row into port at the end of the season.

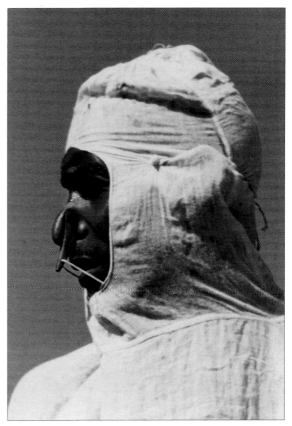

**Far left** A diver rests by holding on to a rope draped over an oar. His bone nose clip can be clearly seen. **Above left** When a diver had reached his limit for staying submerged he was hauled to the surface. If he came up too quickly he could get the 'bends'. **Above** This diver wears a one-piece cotton garment to protect himself from jelly-fish stings. **Left** The oysters were placed in a string bag attached to the diver's hauling line.

**Far left** A well-known Dubai pearl merchant conducting business with a passer-by in the *suq*. Pearls were often kept in pieces of knotted cloth. **Above left** Brass scales were used with polished marble weights and a compendium of sizes, weights and grades. **Above** A pearl merchant on the carpeted deck of his *jelbut*. **Left** Skinning a pearl. This sometimes took place while the pearl was being auctioned, the bids rising as the shape improved.

# HARVESTING
THE SEA

Y DAY, the Gulf was a sea of many hues: green, blue and turquoise, varying with the depth of water and the state of the sky. At night, the slightest agitation brought a show of phosphorescence which dripped from a boat's oars like pearls trickling into the water. Sea snakes glowed in the dark as they wriggled past. Sailors said that only their undersides were luminous, so they swam on their backs in order not to be seen by the large fish in the depths.

As soon as a boat had cleared the shallows, a line would be let out on either side of its stern. From then onwards, a marvellous and varied supply of fish were hauled in. Cooked over a charcoal fire and served on a bed of rice with chopped, raw onions and a good squeeze of lime, they tasted superb. The subject of bait was much discussed. 'Hook up a lime,' said a man from Socotra, 'and a fish will soon join it.'

Fish traps, made either of wire mesh or of closely latticed palm fronds were lowered into the sea near the coast and hauled up and emptied daily. During the winter the majority of people living on the coast caught sprats, which they dried in the sun. These were in demand both in the Shaikhdoms and abroad as animal fodder and fertiliser. Over half the annual catch was exported, which helped to pay for imported foodstuffs such as rice and flour.

There was an immense variety of fish, perhaps two hundred different species, some with bizarre English names: painted grunt, starry blowfish, white spotted guitar fish, bearded mud skipper, penant butterflyfish, Arabian barbed killifish. The Gulf was also a breeding ground for shrimps, though I saw them only in the *suq*, sun-dried and salted. They looked far from appetizing, and a bedu said to me once that he preferred the taste of 'flying shrimps', by which he meant locusts.

A more bizarre product of the sea was ambergris, a dark tar-like substance sometimes found floating in the Gulf, valuable as a base for making perfume. It comes from a secretion of the whale. Once I saw a whale spouting off

Musandam; and twice, along the isolated westermost shore of Abu Dhabi, I found the remains of a sea cow or dungong. This remarkable mammal, over six feet in length, suckles its young on milk, breathes air and has short hairs on its body. Being herbivorous they must have been drawn to the nearby underwater meadows and become grounded while

grazing on them when the tide went out.

Such was the abundance of fish that anyone with the means felt obliged to offer goatmeat or chicken to his guests instead. Only nowadays, when people can afford every kind of food, are they able to relish without inhibition the Gulf's splendid harvest.

**Page 60 and 61** A catch of sprats is spread out to dry in the sun on Jumairah beach. In the background others haul in a large drift-net with another catch. **Above** A fisherman from Jumairah works on a drift-net which when completed and joined to other sections, would be approximately a hundred feet long.

**Left** Hauling in a drift-net. **Below far left** The *gargour* fish trap, some six to eight feet across, was made either of wire or latticed palm fronds. It was lowered into the sea from a boat with bait placed inside and a line attached to a marker float, and emptied every few days. **Below left** Sprats being sorted before being spread on the sand to dry. **Above** A drift-net is closed around its catch and hauled to the shore. This method of fishing was used mainly for catching sprats, which were used either for animal fodder or fertiliser and were one of the Shaikhdoms' main exports.

**Left** A fisherman and boatman from Jumairah.
**Above** A fisherman from Shaam. Dried fish was invaluable as
a foodstuff for the people of the mountains.
A fishmonger **below** cutting up a fish in the *suq* of an inland
market, with his baskets of dried sprats in the foreground.

# THE FALCONER'S ART

WALKING across the salt marshes at the head of Dubai's creek, on a day when the sky was white with humidity and the merging of sky and land broken only by a few shimmering mirages, I noticed a shape moving in the haze. It was a man who had emerged from a hole in the *sabkha* clad only in a loin cloth and with sand clinging to his skin. He stepped forward with dignity. We shook hands.

I knew him – Mohammed, a bedu, sometime pearl-diver, now an itinerant member of the Ruler of Dubai's retinue. But why had he been concealing himself in the ground? He took me to his hide and showed me a spring-trap he had constructed in the hope of catching a falcon which had been seen hovering in the area. The bait was a pigeon attached to a string which would be slowly pulled to the ground when it had been spotted, usually from a great distance, by the falcon. Then, as the falcon alighted, another long string from the hide would release the net.

Several days later, Mohammed appeared at the Ruler's *majlis* carrying a newly-caught falcon. Everyone had some comment to make, the consensus being that it was a good bird in good condition. The Ruler's eldest son, Shaikh Rashid, decided to keep it and rewarded Mohammed generously. Smiling at me, Rashid declared that the bird would be called 'Ingleezi'.

Abdullah, whom I knew as a good shot but not as a falconer, was chosen to train the bird. He laid his rifle and camel stick on the carpet, lifted Ingleezi on to a canvas cuff and began stroking and talking to it. Having flown in from another continent, the bird was now suffering its first day of capitivity. It had been fitted with a hood.

Over the next few weeks the bird and its keeper would seldom be separated. As it began responding to the keeper's voice and taking morsels of fresh meat from his hand, its hood was ever more frequently removed, accustoming the bird to unfamiliar sights, to people and animals. For this reason it would be carried un-hooded through bustling bazaars, the hood being replaced immediately if it became agitated. Whenever I met them, Abdullah's joke was to hood the bird quickly, in case it was frightened by seeing a real Ingleezi.

Taming gave way to training as the bird was taught to fly at a lure of fresh meat tucked inside a bunch of feathers, first on the ground, then whirled in the air. The skill lay in getting the falcon back on the trainer's cuff after each short flight. The ultimate test came when the falcon was let loose to fly at the lure without being attached to a cord.

The last hours before sunset were a favourite time for such training, and I often sat on the sands with one of the Shaikhs, surrounded by a gathering of all his falcons and falconers. Suddenly there was a commotion: one of the falcons had flown off, still wearing its hood. It hovered just above us. 'Quiet,' called the Shaikh, 'so that it can hear its handler.' In vain the falconer called and coo'ed and thumped the ground. The falcon, though unable to see, by chance flew into the top of a palm tree. The handler climbed the tree but, just as he reached the fronds, the hooded bird took fright again and flew off into the desert. The handler followed, returning with the bird two days later, both of them tired and hungry.

The most prized game was the *houbara*, turkey bustard, which crossed the Gulf on its annual migration. Bedu were rewarded by the Shaikhs for bringing news of a *houbara's* sighting. I saw the dramatic arrival of a bedu on a camel which he had not even stopped to saddle. Sliding from his mount he strode into the Ruler's *majlis*; with camel stick held high, he wished 'Peace' on everyone; then violently threw his stick on the carpet and proclaimed he had sighted *houbara*. Orders were given immediately, falconers assembled with their birds, supplies packed, and within a very short time the hunting party was on its way.

At the approach of danger, the *houbara* would lie motionless on the ground. If it was stalked on foot, it would fly off before the hunter came within shooting range: but, once in the air, it became a target for the falcon. The hood was removed and the falcon's dark unblinking eyes would survey the scene. As soon as the falcon sighted its prey the falconer loosed it. The ensuing fight was an exhibition of skill and character, bringing praise or loss of face to the owner and the handler.

Ingleezi, alas, proved a lazy bird. Since our hunting trip happened to be at Christmas, I tried to console her (she was female, but the females, having a longer wing span, are supposed to make the best hunters) with a piece of the tinned Christmas pudding we had brought with us. She declined it. Not a true Ingleezi after all.

**Page 68 and 69** The key to success in falconry is the relationship of falcon and falconer who must exercise patience, skill and devotion. **Below** A falcon on a canvas and leather cuff which protected the falconer's hand from the bird's talons. The bird is unhooded having reached an advanced stage in its training.

**Left** Shaikh Mohammed bin Rashid of Dubai as a child with one of his
father's retainers appointed to teach him the skills of falconry. **Above** Shaikh
Said bin Maktoum, Ruler of Dubai, (grandfather of the boy pictured left)
cuts up meat at a training session on the outskirts of town. A falcon was
rewarded with a titbit of meat for returning to the wrist.

# THE INDISPENSABLE CAMEL

GOD'S GIFT to the bedu, they used to say, was the camel. Without it, man's habitation of the desert would not have been possible. The relationship between man and beast was by no means one-sided, however. The bedu needed camels for transport, milk and occasionally, meat, while the camels were completely dependent on their masters for water, for finding their grazing ground and for assistance in mating.

Up to the middle of this century there were no man-made roads in the Shaikhdoms. A wide barrier of *sabkha* stretched inland from the sea to the beginning of the sands. In summer the glare from its salt obscured the horizon: in winter it became a formidable marsh. Occasionally a camel would break through the thin crust and, in its frantic struggle, either break a leg or became hopelessly trapped, leaving its owner with no choice but to slaughter the beast and, perhaps, carry away its meat on his other camels. This area was known as 'The Devil's Market'.

At the *Maqta'a*, a salt-water ford separating the island of Abu Dhabi from the mainland, camels had a clear advantage over the car, which had to wait for a low tide. Strings of camels travelling to and from the interior could usually cross on all but the highest of tides. At Umm al Nar near the *Maqta'a*, archaeologists unearthed a tombstone, dated around 2700 BC, on which a camel is depicted. This makes it, I believe, the earliest recorded evidence of the camel's presence in Arabia.

On one of my journeys through 'the sands' (as the bedu call the great desert) I met a young herdsman with a few camels. He was far from his people and from any form of help or supplies. His survival kit consisted of a bundle of dried dates and a metal bowl which he wore on his head. The search for grazing had taken him further and further away from the nearest well, which he was circling so as to keep it at least within a couple of days' march. The water from this precious well was so putrid that the bedu would drink it only as a last resort, when it would act on them like a purge. The herdsman had to haul every drop of water some twenty feet to the surface, several times for each camel. The female camels then converted the foul water into a plentiful supply of tasty but creamless milk for his drinking bowl. Apart from dates, these mobile distillation units were his only sustenance.

On another trip, during the intensely hot summer of 1953, I travelled over scorching sands to Suaitiyah, a well under a massive dune at the western extremity of the Liwa. My object was to make contact with a camel party sent there by the Ruler of Abu Dhabi. I saw the

corpses of many camels scattered over the reddish sands. It had been a bad year and the region was devoid of grazing. In their desperate search for a few shoots of vegetation, the owners had taken their camels as far as the poor weak beasts could go before they dropped in their tracks and died.

Arriving at Suaitiyah, I found the situation hardly better; although there was plenty of water from the well, not a handful of grazing remained. The party's fodder was exhausted. The camels were saved – in response to a radioed SOS – by bundles of grass dropped from an RAF plane, based in Sharjah.

The majority of camels in the Shaikhdoms were female, which the bedu preferred for riding. More importantly, they yielded milk. Bull camels were needed only where there were loads to carry; a few were kept as sires, but most of the male calves were slaughtered.

The female produces a single offspring after eleven months' gestation, and suckles it for a year. The young take several years to reach maturity. The life-span of a camel is between 25 and 40 years. It chews the cud like a cow, and is a fastidious feeder, despite enjoying plants which look like barbed wire. The bedu patiently allow their mounts to slow down and, with necks extended, snatch at the grazing as they pass.

The bedu had to be his own vet, scraping the camels' hard skin, tending their wounds and treating them for mange. They were branded with a tribal mark because theft, raiding and disputes about ownership were so frequent.

I remember seeing camels which belonged to the Ruler of Dubai being raced against those of the Ruler of Sharjah. It was effectively a series of point-to-points, with no race track as such, over a distance of about a mile. The start just seemed to happen. Owners and retainers ran for the few available vehicles in which to chase after the contestants. From these mobile grandstands the camels were urged on by shouting, blowing of horns and firing of rifles. This was too much for one of the runners, which turned and charged back into the pursuing stream of supporters. Near the finish, boys ran out to whack their chosen runners on to victory. Amid all the confusion and hilarity it was not always possible to tell who had won.

**Page 76 and 77** A *falaj* at Al Ain – above ground for a while before disappearing into its tunnel – draws its water from the uplands' water table. **Below** This camel train has waited for the low tide to get to the island of Abu Dhabi.

**Left** A bedu from the interior crosses the shallows to Abu Dhabi, his camel laden with its own fodder and palm-frond bags of charcoal for sale in town. **Above** A camel party returning from Abu Dhabi pause to exchange news with travellers from the interior.

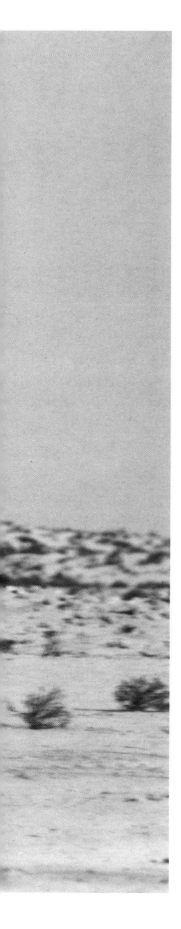

**Left** On special occasions (perhaps as part of some celebration) a camel race was arranged for all-comers. Female camels are much faster than males. One rides on the rump, sometimes with a small saddle, sometimes bareback. **Above** The camel was the bedu's mobile distillation unit converting water into milk, and providing a source of meat, hair and transport. In return bedu were constantly in search of water and grazing for their beasts.

The camel was the bedu's best asset – the camel and the gun. A camel could be used to raise money. A bedu tended his camels with care. **Above** A bedu scrapes away scales and nodules to clear the mange. **Left** A bedu administers medicine.

This *falaj* allowed a camel to be watered at the surface.
Usually water had to be hauled up from wells.

Bedu took it as a right to help themselves to water from any
well and milk from any untended grazing camel. Nonetheless
they slipped off the safety catches on their rifles in case the
camel's owner had a different opinion.

**Left** During an intensely hot summer it was no surprise to find the skeleton of a camel in the desert. It may have died from lack of water or grazing or both.

**Above** Many watchtowers in the vicinity of Al Ain were built to protect the precious *falaj* system.

# THE NOBLE TREE

SHAKESPEARE called it 'the sole Arabian Tree'. The date palm. A symbol of all things good. The mere sight of palm trees breaking a barren skyline or rising from a strip of sandy shore was enough to gladden the traveller's heart. They signified habitation and sweet water. Without them oases would not exist. There is an ancient belief that the first palm tree rose from the residue of the clay out of which Adam was formed.

The palm is said to have its feet in Paradise and its head in Hell – its roots near water, its crown in the fierce sun. Although palms are not difficult to grow, much skill is required in selecting and transplanting young shoots. They are seldom grown from seed because there would be no certainty of a fruit-bearing tree. Palms are male and female, and only the female tree bears fruit. Man's help is needed to arrange satisfactory fertilisation. A male palm of proven record is highly prized, like a stallion.

In spring a shoot or two of the newly opened flower of the male tree is inserted into the newly opened sheath of blossom on the female tree. Alternatively the whole of the male tree's cluster may be taken and its pollen sprinkled over the blossom of many female trees, perhaps forty or sixty: a ratio which indicates the number of male and female palms required.

Just over a month later the fruit begins to appear, small, green and bitter at first, but by midsummer hanging in sizeable clusters among the lower fronds, slowly ripening through shades of amber and red. Some time in August comes a moment of joy when half-ripe dates are picked for savouring, sun-browned and soft on one side, light-amber and crisp on the other. These first fruit of the season would arrive on a Shaikh's tray as a special treat. The rest of the dates remain on the tree until September.

**Previous page** Palms were symbols of life they indicated the presence of sweetish water, shade, food and material for building.

In the old days, no part of a palm tree was wasted. As well as dates, it provided all the materials necessary for a *barasti* hut, with sections of the trunk or the midriff of fronds tied in a bundle to serve as the main supports, around which further fronds were tied with rope made from palm fibre to form the walls and roof. Other fronds made fences against the encroaching sand dunes. Leaves were woven into baskets and mats. Date stones were used as fodder for camels and goats or for making charcoal. Palm fibre might be pushed into the spout of a coffee-pot to act as a filter, or into a gun barrel to keep out sand. Palm fronds were lashed together and shaped into the *shasha*, the canoe with a bark-filled compartment to provide buoyancy.

It was announced a few years ago in the United Arab Emirates that 15th September would in future be known as Arab Palm Day. A fitting tribute to a noble tree.

**Below and left** Palm trunks were used to construct hoists over wells for irrigating palm groves. Water was hauled to the surface by an ox driven down a ramp. These wells were in areas where there was fodder for the oxen. **Above** At harvest time either whole clusters of dates were cut or, if for immediate consumption, single near-ripe dates picked, often brown and soft only on the side the sun had caught.

A *shasha*, a canoe of palm fronds still in use on the eastern shore of the Shaikhdoms, was probably the first type of craft in the Arabian Gulf in ancient times. The keel of the *shasha* was an enclosure stuffed with palm bark for extra buoyancy.

**Above** The trunk and fronds of the palms provided most building material for houses and dwellings – the *khaima* (tent), or *arish*, or *barasti*. Such homes were cheap, easily built and cool. Sections of palm trunks were sometimes used as the main supports. **Right** Shoots of palm trees with a good record of date bearing were much prized. These cuttings had been carefully carried by camel from Oman for planting at one of the Liwa oases.

# SWEET WATER

THE BARREN LANDS of the Shaikhdoms were rendered habitable only by accumulations of sweet water lying unseen beneath their arid sand masses and gravel plains. With few exceptions, every drop needed had to be hauled manually from hand-dug wells. More often than not their names were the only features shown on the map of a desert region. In remote areas they might be wholly or partially closed by blown sand, and had to be cleared before use. Their presence was revealed by a surrounding area of darkened sand and scattered camel droppings.

A bedu approached a well with caution, his experienced eye searching for signs of recent visitors. After clearing its head, he would construct a portable trough and then begin the hard work of hauling up the water in a goatskin bucket. His loaded rifle was kept within easy reach. Occasionally the water proved so salty or putrid that unless he was desperate, he wouldn't drink it, and even the camels would drink only after he had closed their nostrils. When these tasks were completed, he would retire to the surrounding dunes, safely away from the well, which might be visited by marauders.

Such lonely wells frequently bore the name of the first traveller to have dug them. The remains of some solitary excavator were found in one of the shafts, the sides having collapsed on him. Digging wells in soft sand was a hazardous business for a lone traveller.

At the other extreme were much more elaborate wells with enough water to support settlement, palm groves and, perhaps, small scale agriculture. A tripod of palm trunks made them visible from a distance. Rigged over a well, the palm trunks carried a pulley through which a rope was passed. The rope was attached to an ox or an ass which could be driven down a ramp precisely as long as the well was deep. This hauled to the surface an enormous skin scoop. Another rope tilted the scoop to pour water into a trough, from which it was directed into a maze of irrigation channels.

The nights I spent trying to sleep in palm groves irrigated by such wells resounded with incessant noise. 'Ough!' cried the operator when, with a whack of a frond, he would turn the ox and drive it down the ramp. Then came the creak of the wooden pulley, the groan of a wooden spindle, the protest of ropes and rig taking the strain of the heavy scoop. A splash as the water was tipped into the trough. 'Ough!' cried the operator as he turned the ox and they began to climb the ramp again. Under less strain, the apparatus squeaked at a higher pitch as the scoop went down. 'Ough!' came the cry, as man and beast turned once more to begin another cycle. The music continued throughout the night, accompanied periodically by voices from the grove noisily discussing the opening and closing of the irrigation channels.

The biggest desert wells, situated in areas of comparatively good grazing, boasted proper well-heads and troughs of stone and gypsum. They were focal points of desert life where news was exchanged as the visitors worked. At peak times their use had to be maximised, rendering it incumbent on everyone to work swiftly. Hand over hand, skin buckets of water were hauled up, emptied into a trough and then quickly dropped back down the well. The haulers were relieved as soon as they became tired. Camels drank some four or five buckets of water each.

Much of the hauling was accompanied by a chant, sometimes the same as sailors used when hauling on their sails. The next impatient group would move in closer to the well, taunting those already there. Amid the shouting and non-stop chatter, elderly women squatted and spun cotton. Goatskins were filled and loaded on to donkeys. Herds were disentangled and a gaggle of people and animals wended off into the desert, leaving the activity at the well undiminished.

Some parts of the Shaikhdoms had – and still do obtain – water not only from wells but through the remarkable *falaj* system of ducts, constructed long ago to tap the water table at the foot of the Hajar mountains for the benefit of cultivable land in the plains. Using only

primitive tools, the diggers chipped through rock to create a gently descending underground watercourse of ducts and chambers for thousands of feet to where it was needed. The route could be traced above ground by the line of open shafts through which the excavated soil and rock had been lifted, and which served to ventilate the channels and provide access for cleaning and maintenance. Settlements grew according to the amount of agriculture their *falaj* systems could sustain. Forts and watchtowers had been built to keep guard over them and their precious water supply.

Water-carrying was a thriving business in some of the coastal towns, where donkeys laden with containers of up to sixteen gallons were constantly seen trotting to and from outlying wells. Their riders had hauled the water up and

**Page 98 and 99** Water is poured into a bowl often borne on the head under the headcloth.
**Above left** Earthenware water pots are porous, the dry air cools their contents.
**Above right** Wells in areas of good grazing were the principal meeting places in the desert.

would sell it after transporting it to town. At low tide, water donkeys splashed out through the shallows to vessels preparing for sea. A member of the crew would sample the water before it was tipped into the ship's skin-lined wooden tank – in case the seller had cheated by drawing unpalatable water from some nearby well, which the crew would then have to drink throughout the voyage.

At most wells water had to be hauled up by hand, but in some palm groves **left** an ox was employed. The wooden pulleys of the contraption created a distinctive 'well music' which could be heard from afar. From a goatskin bucket hauled up from the well **above**, water cascades into the irrigation channel.

**Top left** For want of a cup a bedu drinks straight from the goatskin at a well-head. **Left** At Umm al Zamul, the well had to be cleared of sand before it deserved its name. Today the boundaries of three countries converge there – the United Arab Emirates, the Kingdom of Saudi Arabia and the Sultanate of Oman. A father **above** douches his son with well-water. Even in the heat of summer the water was surprisingly cold.

A water well in Abu Dhabi. Brackish water was frequently filtered through a corner of a headcloth to reduce impurities.

# THE LIWA

NTIL ALMOST the middle of this century, one of the most important areas of Abu Dhabi territory, on the north-eastern limits of the Empty Quarter, was either not shown on maps at all, or was indicated by a single name representing a wide scatter of oases enfolded by high dunes – the Liwa. The paramount Shaikh of the principal tribe, the Bani Yas, lived there up to 1792, when he moved to a newly founded coastal settlement called Abu Dhabi, which subsequently gave its name to the whole State.

Wilfred Thesiger, in the late 1940s, was the first to map and describe for the outside world this long straggling group of some sixty oases nestled among mountainously high dunes. He urged me to see the Liwa for myself.

Eventually I made the first motor reconnaissances of the great sands – four expeditions, lasting weeks at a time. They were uncertain journeys, in scorching heat, not without hardship and danger. But they did not qualify for Thesiger's approval, for he believed that the only true way to gain a feel for the country was to plod through it on foot or camel. During those first journeys, before the arrival of large smooth tyres and specially adapted vehicles, there were stretches when camels would indeed have been a faster and more reliable form of transport.

Where one left the coastal *sabkha* and headed south for the Liwa depended on which oasis one was aiming for and on the preferences and knowledge of the bedu guides. They had a different term for every feature of the desert, no

**Previous page** Viewed south from the Liwa, the smooth flanks of giant dunes conceal the steep slopes beyond their brinks. A well or even a settlement might lie between dunes, and an expert guide was needed to find them. In this fearsome environment of the largest sand mass in the world, the bedu could survive on his camels, a well and perhaps a few dates from an oasis . . . and his absolute faith in God.

matter how slight, enabling them to describe a route or place, according to the nature of the sand or types of plant.

Gradually the white sand began to form low unconnected dunes, among which lay a straggling line of wells, dug about twenty miles from the coast to which they were parallel. This was the Bainunah where families and camels could be left while the menfolk walked to the shore to go fishing or to fetch supplies by boat from Abu Dhabi town. South of these wells, the sand continued to deepen and the dunes to merge.

Coarse grains reddened the heightening dunes, which then quite suddenly gave way to a smooth undulating belt where vehicles could move at greater speed – until they arrived unexpectedly at the brink of a steep dune several hundred feet high. Braking heavily on soft sand was effective, for the vehicle sank immediately to rest on its chassis, possibly with its front overhanging the drop. Then the only way was down.

Descending the steep face of such a dune was a sensational experience. At an angle of 33 degrees from the perpendicular, one looked into a hollow 600 feet below. The best steerage was obtained from a steady speed, whereas the natural tendency, at first, was to go slowly, foot by foot, causing a muffled creaking sound which grew louder in the intense heat and was amplified by the crescent shape of the dune. If the descent was on to the back of another dune, the bottom would be at a sharp angle, and the approach had to be slow enough to avoid heavy impact, yet fast enough for a climb up the slope ahead without getting stuck.

Guides would scan the bleak landscape, looking for recognisable features; in an area of big dunes, away from the well-to-well routes, the best they could do was maintain a general sense of direction. They seldom gave directions verbally, but flicked their hands to left or right, as if steering a camel by tapping its neck.

To arrive suddenly at the edge of a dune and see a well in the hollow below, particularly in the extreme heat of summer, stirred the kind of joy that made a man want to fire his rifle in exaltation. A welcome sight indeed when the sands were so hot that even the bedu protected their tough feet with long goats' hair socks, which they knitted themselves.

The Liwa comprised many small pockets of palm groves and *barasti* houses stretched across an area, some seventy-five miles wide, of dramatic sand dunes bordering the Empty Quarter. The Liwa group comprised about 60 oases, forming an east-west crescent. They ranged from a single clump of palm trees to large groves with many huts on the surrounding dunes.

Those whose lives centred on the oases had to augment their scant living by fishing, pearl diving and grazing their camels. It was a lifestyle of extreme contrasts. At one time they were alone in the great sea of sand, where the air was so dry that the night skies were crammed with stars right down to the horizon, and the quiet was so profound that you could hear a date fall from the palm: at other times they were diving beneath a crowded boat groping for oysters, where the humidity above the sea was so dense that it robbed the sky of any blue, and, at night, blotted out all the stars except those immediately overhead.

Only the old, the sick and the very young remained in the Liwa the whole year round, but, unless they were pearl diving, most owners of palm trees returned for the date harvest. *Barasti* houses which had been empty for much of the year would then be occupied. Some would have filled with sand, which had to be pushed out, or the *barasti* might have to be re-erected elsewhere.

The desert held more wildlife than I at first expected. Scarabs would be seen on the sands, near wells, constantly rolling camel droppings to their nests. Twice I was visited by snakes. I spotted a chameleon and a lone grasshopper. But the bleached skeletons of camels were a grim reminder of the precarious balance between survival and death.

Occasionally the sands themselves would groan, like the mythical bellowing of some giant or the sound of a low-flying, piston-engined aircraft roaring is perhaps the best description. I heard this strange phenomenon only during the afternoons of intensely hot days in summer at the base of giant dunes.

Any food except camels' milk, dates, and occasional game, was a luxury which had to be fetched from afar, mainly from Abu Dhabi, a trip entailing an absence of more than a week. The return to his oasis of someone who had been on such a visit gave rise to much excitement as his family unloaded the camels, taking charge of the new supply of foodstuffs and searching hopefully for presents.

Although they lived on the edge of that great void, the Empty Quarter, they frequently needed the security of a gun, for fear of audacious bandits emerging from the sands. The remoteness of the oases was beyond mere mileage. There were no hospitals or doctors to whom the people of the Liwa could travel, not even in Abu Dhabi town, and no relief for the suffering of the sick, except a few folk remedies, other than their own spiritual strength. Their lives were hard, but their endurance was great and their belief in God absolute. In their own eyes, they were neither rich nor poor, fatalistically accepting hardship without complaint, yet quick in gratitude to their Maker for His blessings.

On the crest of a dune to survey the route ahead, this barefoot guide **left** spares one foot the burning heat of the sand. The soles of the feet might be thick and insensitive enough, but not the upper skin on to which the scorching soft sand would pour. Because of the burning sand, these tribesmen **above** came down the steep face of a 600-foot sand dune at Arada in the western Liwa like men on the attack. **Below** A sand dune deeply scarred by camel tracks.

**Facing page:** The tents of bedu on the move **top left** were little more than improvised awnings woven from palm leaves. **Top right** Houses would sometimes fill with sand during a long absence by the owners, as this family found when it returned by camel from Abu Dhabi. **Left** Liwa oases ranged from large, permanent settlements with sizeable palm groves on salt-flats to small clusters of huts beside a few palms in the hollows of the dunes, occupied only at harvest-time. Dwellings were usually sited on low-lying dunes above the palm trees. **This page:** With the glare of the sun and the constant blowing of dust and sand, many bedu suffered burning eyelids (conjunctivitis). Rubbing with anything cool, such as a snake's tail **above left**, brought relief. Some bedu painted their eyelids with *kohl*, which was said to be beneficial. **Above right** A bunch of barely ripe dates is produced for travellers in the shelter of this Liwa *barasti* home.

# TRAVELLERS
# FROM AFAR

ON CAMELS from afar occasionally would come small parties of tribesmen or lone bedu. Most of the time they lived in the sands and plains fringing the great Empty Quarter, into which they would sometimes wander in search of grazing or to escape from enemies. Frontiers had not been drawn; they regarded the whole of the south-eastern corner of the Arabian peninsula as their birthright. They roamed in places where mere survival was an achievement, but, because of their constant communion with God, they never felt alone.

When the fancy took them, they might make the long journey to one of the populated centres on the shores of the Gulf. For some it would be their first glimpse of the sea. When they arrived in one of the Shaikhdoms, the visitors would call on the Shaikh and casually attach themselves to his entourage, for having left their means of subsistence in the desert, they were dependent on whatever hospitality they found. How they were received depended on the visitors' personal standing and whether the Shaikh wished to maintain an alliance with their tribe.

They would feel at ease among the Shaikh's retainers who, like themselves, were of tribal origin. They were apt to be less popular among the more settled townsfolk, to whom an armed visitor seemed a potential threat. Moreover, settled people were irked by the overbearing, aristocratic, attitude of the bedu whom they regarded as being aimless and poor. Conversely, the bedu thought little of the townees, with whom their main contact was in the market place where standards and values were different. Soon, they might wish themselves back where the ownership of camels counted more than the possession of paper money.

Within a few days, the novelty and attractions of the town had waned. The visiting nomads would seek news of the desert from other travellers. Then, suddenly, they would be gone, often without so much as a goodbye. To the desert traveller, it was the meeting and greeting that mattered, not the farewell.

With their alert eyes, long hair, lean bodies and militant appearance, these men from the distant sands were a fine subject for my camera. Nor were they camera shy – though one bedu, with his own ideas on how to pose, kept pointing his rifle at the camera, finally firing a shot over my head to liven up what, to him, would otherwise have been dull proceedings.

The Al Rashid were typical of the men from the southern sands. I was introduced to them by a traveller no less picturesque, Wilfred Thesiger, known as 'Mubarak bin London' (the Blessed One, Son of London), famous for his crossings of the Empty Quarter.

One evening, a small group of weary Al Rashid hammered at my door in Dubai. They gently pushed to their fore a stocky man with bright eyes recessed in a deeply wrinkled face, introducing him as Salih bin Kalut. We talked for a long time; he was alert and friendly. Later that evening I learned that he was in such pain that, on the long journey from the south, his companions (who included one of his sons) had tied him across his camel, because he couldn't keep upright.

I was deeply touched when Salih thanked me for my friendship with his people. He regarded me as being of the same tribe as Thesiger; an honour indeed.

Another notable explorer, Bertram Thomas, who had been the first to cross the Empty Quarter, wrote of Salih in 1932:

. . . he bore the magic name of bin Kalut – Kalut, the most famous lady in all the sands, daughter of a famous warrior, and mother of three warrior sons, for to have kindred who destroy their enemies (and cleave to their friends) is the very essence of nobility in this environment.

Showing me some of his scars, Salih told me that he had been wounded twenty-six times. Now, he was terminally ill, and nothing could be done for him, but he bore his pain as bravely as he had borne his wounds, with silent

Shaikh Salih bin Kalut.
**Page 116 and 117** The bedu have travelled to the Shaikhdoms
from the southern fringes of the Empty Quarter.

suffering, the surest symbol of manhood. His mother, the great Kalut, would have been proud of him.

He died in Dubai a few days later on 15th December 1953. His well worn body was washed and swathed in the cloth of a pilgrim, and carried a short distance from town, and laid to rest before sunset in the sand near Al Fahidi Fort. There were no stones available, so a dis-carded cooking pot was pushed into the sand at his head, which was pointing properly towards Mecca. It had probably been used before for the same purpose, and would be dislodged by a strong gust of wind.

Next morning, their duty done, the men from the Al Rashid left on their long trek south, with Salih's now riderless camel trailing behind on a halter.

**Left** Two Salims of the Al Rashid tribe – on the left, bin Kabina and on the right, bin Ghubaisha – they were companions of Wilfred Thesiger on most of his journeys in south-eastern Arabia. They are photographed here on a visit to the Shaikhdoms where bin Ghubaisha was shortly to establish a reputation as a brigand. Every tribesman was armed **above**, although few possessed modern rifles. Raids and tribal feuds kept everyone in a constant state of alertness. Often on desert journeys the only meat eaten was game bagged with the gun.

A bedu of the Manasir tribe in the Liwa. Bedu either kept
their heads shaved or wore their hair very long and
sometimes plaited.

The late Ali bin Thamir, the famous guide in the desert
regions of Abu Dhabi.

**Far left and left** Wilfred Thesiger, one of the foremost explorers and travellers of this century (below photographed after his 1949-1950 travels in Oman). He was known among his tribal companions as Mubarak bin London. He made several crossings of the Empty Quarter desert and was the first westerner to explore extensively and map the Liwa group of oases. **Above** Salim bin Ghubaisha, following the custom of many members of the Al Rashid tribe, bore the name of his mother.

Before returning to the interior this bedu **above** sees a
fortune-teller. She tells his future by casting pieces of shell
and stones on the sand and then reading their pattern. His
rifle is protected by a goatskin cover. **Right** Salim bin
Ghubaisha, with a gazelle reared by the author and his wife.

# THE
# CAMEL'S SUCCESSOR

WHEN I LIVED in the Shaikhdoms we reckoned distance in travel time, not mileages: time was only approximate. Camels were still the main means of transport. There were very few motor vehicles: and, although these increased sharply during the various phases of oil exploration, during seasonal work by the anti-locust organisation and after the creation of a small levy force, people could still recognise them individually.

As there were no roads, there were no traffic regulations and no agreement as to which side vehicles should pass each other. The usable track might be half a mile wide but accidents occurred generally when vehicles closed in to identify each other and collided head-on. While being driven at speed to get through the soft sand, they had been known to hit boats pulled up on the shore, and to have become stuck on the beach at low tide or submerged at high tide.

The most suitable vehicle for light, off-the-track work, was the Jeep, superseded by the four-wheel drive Land Rover, which first reached the Shaikhdoms around 1950. The early model, with its short wheel-base and small tyres, nevertheless gave an uncomfortable ride, and it was frequently immobilised by the intense heat, which caused a leakage of oil on to the clutch plate. Later models, once those faults had been overcome and with a larger wheel-base, constituted a superb workhorse for the Shaikhdoms.

Like a ship at sea, a vehicle going into the interior had to be self-sufficient in supplies and resources. 'Chinko' (that is, PSPs, or – Perforated Steel Plates) became a familiar Arabic term. A couple of strips carried on a vehicle, particularly if it was only two-wheel drive, were invaluable. Hot sand had to be scooped from under the rear wheels so that the tyres could grip the 'Chinko' when pushed under them. The process might need repeating every few yards. We were often so exhausted by 'Chinkoing' that we camped and waited for the sands to cool at night – which upset the calculation of travel-time.

The state of the sand made a tremendous difference. Worst was the fine white sand when dry and very hot, best was the orange-red sand when cool or damp from a heavy dew. There was a huge variation in the 'firming' of the sand between sunset and dawn.

It was usually prudent to rely, for choice of route, on a bedu guide, who knew the country and could maintain a general sense of direction, the role of the driver being simply to avoid obvious difficulties and not get stuck. If all went well it was good fun, but there was always a danger of suddenly going over the edge of a dune at the wrong angle and rolling downhill, as I did on two occasions.

The salt flats could be very difficult to traverse. When dry they provided a good, fast surface for motoring, although the uncertain crust might break, opening into a bog-like mass in which one's vehicle would stick. In winter the surface might be covered with water, from rain or an exceptionally high tide or seepage from below, making it slippery and concealing the holes left where other vehicles had been dug out.

In the coastal areas there seemed far more tyre tracks than vehicles, but they might be up to twenty years old, dating back to the arrival of the first car. On the other hand, tracks might be obliterated by drifting sand within an hour or so. The same vehicle passing several times over the same track would leave what appeared to be a much used route. I learned never to sleep near car tracks at night, knowing that another vehicle might follow them.

In 1950 Shaikh Rashid bin Said of Dubai made one of the first big motor journeys from the Shaikhdoms. He went overland on the Pilgrimage to Mecca. For its day, it was an epic journey and a tribute to the ingenuity of his mainly self-taught driver-mechanics, who kept the wheels of the old vehicles turning.

When there were sufficient passengers, a few enterprising taxi owners were prepared to drive from the coastal towns of the eastern seaboard as far as Muscat. I travelled in a Model

'T' Ford, precariously kept going by the ingenuity of its driver. Another vehicle in this antiquated fleet had a badly leaking radiator on which was prominently mounted an easily visible water temperature gauge. Passengers and goats having been loaded, we would lurch forward for a couple of miles until the needle in the gauge pointed to the red area. Then we would all off-load; the goat resumed its grazing while the driver, carrying a battered petrol tin, went in search of water.

Even if one had an uneventful journey across the salt flats, the ford separating Abu Dhabi island from the mainland could be crossed only at low tide. Even then winds and currents could render it impassable. The problem was finally overcome by the construction of a stone causeway. The builder, Khan Sahib Hussain Amad, erected a sign on it which said: 'Slow'. This was the first public traffic sign in the Shaikhdoms.

**Page 128 and 129** The first Land Rover to reach the Shaikhdoms makes its descent from a rolling sand dune on the first motor journey to the Liwa. Shortly after this picture was taken the Land Rover rolled over down a high dune but was eventually righted. **From the top** The *sabkha* in winter was hazardous to cross at high tide, a film of water oozes through the crust. All hands assist a two-wheel-drive pick-up up a dune, crossing the Ramlat Annaij. When a vehicle breaks through the *sabkha* there is trouble.

A motorable route was found through the
Wadi al Qor from the western to the eastern
coast.

The approach to the Wadi al Qor across a
gravel plain near Jebel Faiyah. The camel
party was from the Batinah coast. Camels had
more routes open to them than motors.

**Above** A stone causeway was eventually built to cross the *Maqta'a* to Abu Dhabi island. Travellers were no longer dictated to by the state of the tides.
**Below** This ex-RAF lorry was used as a taxi from Sharjah to the eastern coast. It had to carry enough petrol and its passengers enough food and drink for a journey of several days.

**Above** The author at the wheel of an early Land Rover,
accompanied by members of the Habus tribe of Ras al Khaima.
**Below** An elderly taxi plied the route along the Batinah coast
from Muscat as far north as was drivable.

# MOUNTAIN MEN

ERY FEW PEOPLE of the Shaikhdoms travelled, other than by sea, outside the immediate area in which they lived. There were no formal boundaries, but the whole of southeastern Arabia was a maze of different spheres of influence, over which the Ruling Shaikhs and tribal leaders exercised varying degrees of control. Travel to the hinterland was difficult and hazardous. And there was one area into which not even the boldest traveller cared to venture – the rugged and barren Musandam Peninsula.

It was not the mountains which people feared, grim though they were, but their inhabitants, generally known as the Shihuh. Ancient stories presented the Shihuh as wild men, servants of the Evil Spirits. Parents would threaten their children: 'Be good or the Shihuh will come and get you.'

They lived where the Hajar range of mountains tumbles into the broken peninsula at the neck of the Arabian Gulf, forming an outline very familiar to passing mariners. Those waters have recently become one of the most important maritime channels in the world – the Strait of Hormuz; oil tankers now dot a horizon once broken only by the lateen sails of Arab vessels plying to India and East Africa.

Before the drawing of frontiers, sovereignty over this remote corner of Arabia was never clear. The tip of the peninsula belonged to the Sultanate of Oman, but over the years many pieces of land where the Shihuh lived came to be seen by the Shaikhdoms as theirs. It was, and is, a confusing patchwork.

Political frontiers meant little, anyway, to the people of the hills, concerned only with their access to water, their scant food supplies and their migration patterns.

The mountains themselves are barren rock and yield less grazing than sandy desert. Here and there small plots hold just enough soil to make cultivation possible. Some of these are so difficult to reach and so precariously perched that the Shihuh had to pull their makeshift ploughs themselves. Camels are quite unsuited to the terrain and donkeys need grazing which the highlands do not provide. Goats were the main livestock, but only in such numbers as the scant grazing could support. Only scraggy chickens were able to find something to feed on.

The Shihuh depended for water on small ancient cisterns hollowed out of the rock. In the high summer when all the cisterns were dry, they migrated to coves and coastal strips, where they fished or tended date palms. Friction often ensued. Because they lived among such steep gullies in the mountains, the Shihuh had little cohesiveness as a tribe. Each clan was isolated in its own fastness, linked only to the sites of its coastal migrations.

Any attempt by a stranger to enter the Shihuh's territory was met by shrill cries from unseen figures, sounding the alarm from one hilltop to another. It was an uncanny noise, reverberating through the hostile hills. Eventually those who had created it would emerge into view, leaping across the boulders and brandishing their little axes. Others, appearing against the skyline of the surrounding hills, created the false impression that the mountains were densely inhabited. To have approached them would have confirmed their fears. The wise plan was to sit in the *wadi* and form a *majlis*. Then the hillmen would slowly and cautiously come near and establish contact.

The isolation of the Shihuh over many centuries had produced differences in appearance, customs and language. They were distinguished by their unusual axes; tiny, one-by two-and-a-half inch axe-heads mounted on disproportionately large wooden handles. These were used as weapons, tools and clambering sticks. Their daggers were different too, short straight blades, less ornate than the traditional curved *khanjar* of Arabia but more practical. On their belts the Shihuh often carried a small semi-circular leather pouch, sometimes faced with silver, containing the key to a store-cum-house high in the mountains, where their precious grain was kept. Swords and flintlock rifles, being an encumbrance, were carried only

**Page 136 and 136** Shihuh tribesmen position themselves along the cliff tops to observe the movements of visitors through the *wadi* beneath. **Above** Parts of the Musandam Peninsula are extremely precipitous and many of the mountain paths unsuited to pack animals. Tribesmen carried all their supplies up the mountains by hand, and they themselves pulled their own ploughs on their small plots of cultivable land.

when they expected to meet strangers. Anything that could be used was highly prized – a toilet chain with its ceramic handle, which became a belt and key chain, or a table knife from a P & O liner sharpened to a dagger point.

A strange custom had survived among the Shihuh perhaps from pre-Islamic times. They called it the *nadaba* or *qubub*. A group of them would cluster about their cheer-leader who held a goat's head or skull above him, with which he seemed to beat time, while uttering a curious howl of changing pitch, accompanied by a chorus of deep grunts from the surrounding group. Strongly rhythmic rather than melodious, it was an eerie thing to hear, deep in the mountains and at night.

Whatever the origin of this custom, its modern practitioners used it mainly to show their appreciation of a special meal. The killing and eating of a goat was an event worthy to be broadcast throughout the locality, and the unusual sound of the *nadaba* carried the message far along the *wadis* and over the mountain ridges.

Another curious custom was intended as a symbolic test of enthusiasm for a Shihi bridegroom. The bride stayed inside her dwelling, with a close male relative stationed at the entrance, holding a club or axe handle. He would strike the groom as he rushed inside to claim his bride. The majority of the Shihuh married the daughters of their paternal uncles; but the more distant the relationship between bride and groom, the harder the blow.

Poor Shihuh. Theirs was the aggressiveness of the fearful – fearful less for their bodily safety than for their meagre stocks of water, grain and livestock. They occupied some of the grimest inhabited terrain on earth. There were seasons when they came so close to starvation that the smallest threat to their supplies was a threat to life. Until they could be sure that intruders were peaceful – and provisioned – they confronted them on the assumption that they might have to fight or perish. So their unique wilderness remained as unexplored as when Nearchus, commanding Alexander the Great's fleet, nosed into the Gulf in 325 BC.

A tribesman on watch over one of the many bays of
the Musandam Peninsula.

Heaped and unhewn stones were used for storage, penning
goats and defensive pill-boxes. Rifles were of various
vintages, mostly antique muskets. Those with a modern rifle
had probably obtained it through service with one of the
Rulers.

**Above** The Shihuh differed in appearance from the people of the plains and desert, and their springy axe and straight dagger were their unique characteristic. The little leather pouch (silver-faced in the picture) usually contained a key to a store-house. Firearms were carried only when strangers were at hand. **Right** A Shihuh waves his axe aloft, here in greeting, but often as a warning to an unwanted visitor.

# BUSTLING BAZAARS

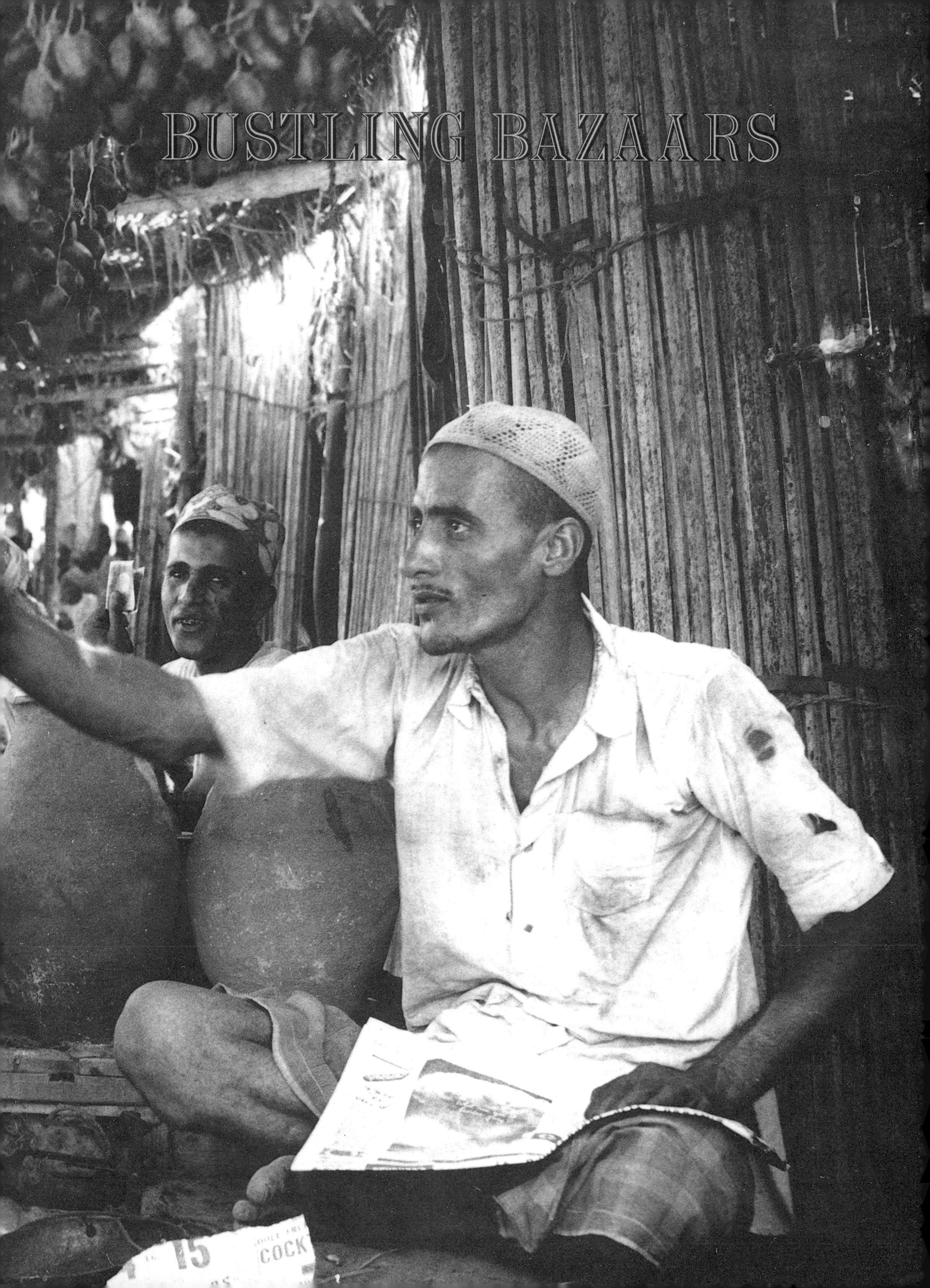

EVERY SMALL TOWN or substantial village along the seaboard of the Shaikhdoms, and some of the inland settlements as well, had a *suq* – a market place or bazaar. Although varying greatly in size, each was of crucial importance to the people it served. Sea routes and camel trails converged on them from many directions. Armed tribesmen and sailors, settled people and travellers of every description, seemed to circulate in them endlessly, coming and going like the tide, a bustling microcosm of human activity.

The *suq* might appear just a disorganised adjunct of the town, but could actually have been the origin of the town itself. Darkened by the ceaseless passage of feet and hooves, its sandy floor would be so hard that rain lingered in puddles. Merchants improvised shelters from palm fronds and, if they prospered, built little open-fronted booths of coral and gypsum secured at night with wooden shutters. Awnings of fronds dappled the narrow lanes between the shops, while here and there, some enterprising traders had improvised a wind-tower from a frame of mangrove poles covered with sackcloth.

The layout of the *suq* was not planned, but had evolved over the centuries out of practical considerations. Merchants and artisans of the same trade tended to set up business alongside each other, forming specialist areas. Fish were unloaded and sold on the outskirts, as were livestock and timber and stacks of mangrove poles. In the blacksmiths' and pot makers' sector there was a continual noise of hammering – which suddenly stopped as one entered the strangely silent area of the cloth sellers. Here a forest of cottons and silks hanging in drapes or piled high in rolls, muffled all sounds except the flip-flop of sandals and the hum of a sewing machine. Round another corner, the heady aroma of spices and herbs blended into a pungent bouquet. So distinct were the sounds and smells of the *suq* that a blind beggar told me he never had the slightest difficulty in finding his way through the labyrinth of alleyways.

A bedu, squatting beside a letter-writer one hand on his rifle, the other uneasily tugging at his beard, sought inspiration. '*Ya Korani*,' he would exclaim, 'tell them, tell them that Abdullah greets them. Tell them . . .' A short distance away the *nakhuda* of a *boom* stood before another scribe, his defiant stance and gestures indicating the angry tenor of the letter he was dictating. Further along, a Shaikh sat on the platform in front of a grocer's booth, with a circle of people around him, as he adjudicated a dispute.

Not much was needed to start up in business. A porter whose back had been injured arrived one day with a frying pan, primus stove and a disused petrol tin full of a brown dough-like substance which he shaped into round cakes and fried. He did brisk business, for he had seen a gap in the market – the feeding of hungry porters. Another porter bought a razor and a pair of scissors and set up in business beside him as a barber; clients were usually sold one of the fried cakes as their beards were trimmed or heads shaven. The Shaikhdoms with no currency of their own used the silver Indian rupee, although the silver Maria Theresa dollar of 1780 was always acceptable. Beard trimming cost four annas, a quarter of a rupee. In 1948, a *suq* porter earned about two rupees a day. Nine pounds of rice cost seven rupees.

Three cheerful ladies sat in a row under my verandah, selling any odds and ends that came their way, mostly from my house. Bottles, tins, film containers (useful for holding dried and chopped local tobacco), old copies of the *Airmail Times* (good for wrapping), scraps of wire and string, small bundles of grass, candle stubs and buttons.

The *suq* contained many surprises. One itinerant trader agreed to make me a pair of pyjamas for my forthcoming honeymoon. The result was a splendid Chinese silk replica of a double-breasted suit complete with wallet pockets, turn-ups and a large array of unmatching buttons, including four on each cuff.

**Page 144 and 145** In season, fresh dates were a welcome sight. They were
sold all year round pressed in baskets. **Above** An enormous variety of goods
could be on offer at one stall.

After the austerity of a long desert journey a bedu visitor would come eagerly to the *suq*. He would approach with a swagger, camel stick in hand, fresh kohl around his eyes, long hair pushed up into his cashmere headcloth. His rifle (except where rifles were banned from the *suq*) would be carried horizontally across his shoulder, with belts of ammunition crossed over his chest and around his lean waist, and in front an impressive curved dagger. His superior manner would soon give way to sheer delight at the wealth of goods. Although tempted by some novelty, he would bargain carefully for the ordinary objects that were so needed in the desert – a cooking or coffee pot, rope, a knife, a dish, a headcloth, a length of material for his family, and basic foodstuffs. If an expensive item such as a new *khanjar* caught his eye, he might seek a fellow tribesman and try to borrow money or sell him a camel.

Around sunset lanterns were lit in each of the little open-fronted shops. The lamplight created a warm and cosy glow, but threw sinister shadows on to the bearded faces peering at the merchandise. Eventually shutters were fastened, shoppers went home or back to their boats, and the shopkeepers also departed carrying the lighted lanterns. Even the beggars ceased to plead. The only signs of life came from a watchman swinging his hurricane lamp, and the constant scurrying of rats. The *suq* was closed.

**Left** An itinerant bookbinder. Such craftsmen travelled from port to port carrying the tools of their trade in boxes on which they set up their business. When they had exhausted the local need for their skills, they moved on. **Above** At one time or another many people, such as this *nakhuda* (standing), would require the help of a scribe – sometimes a well-disposed merchant, but usually a professional letter-writer.

People of different nationalities and origins, speaking many languages, established themselves as shopkeepers in the *suqs*, particularly along the coast. **Above** A shopkeeper whiles away a slack time smoking a water-pipe. Most of the goods seen in this picture were for urban dwellers and seamen rather than bedu. Hurricane or pressure lamps **right** were used to light the stalls at night. When the wooden shutters were pulled across these open-fronted booths, the shopkeepers would use their lanterns to light their way home. **Far right** Two traders chat while waiting for customers. A large bowl at the front of the shop holds *halwa* – a sweetmeat.

**Above** At the cloth stall purchases varied from a length to a whole bolt, some of which was carried for re-sale to inland settlements or to markets across the Gulf. **Top right** A young man takes his siesta surrounded by his wares, on site at his father's stall. **Right** Women often sold produce obtained by their husbands. This woman and her daughter are selling charcoal.

FESTIVE DRUMS

IT WAS HOT and humid. Normally there would have been no need for the little charcoal fires except to brew coffee. But this was not a normal day; a celebration was pending and the fires were needed to dry and tighten the skins of the drums. On this occasion the son of a Shaikh and some of the boy's friends were to be circumcised: but it might equally well have been a wedding or one of the two major religious festivals, Eid al Fitr and the Eid al Adha, for the pattern was always much the same although the scale differed.

A place would be chosen near the town or village. A flag was hoisted – usually that of the Shaikhdom, but sometimes any piece of coloured material. After further warming the large bass drum was set in the sand, while hand-drums and tambourines were held over the embers. Then a loud rhythmic banging of the large drum sent out a general summons. People converged from many directions, with them other small groups of drummers and musicians each gathering under its own banner.

I remember the rhythm of the drums, large and small, growing faster. Flutes and cymbals joined in and the paid entertainers who formed the nucleus of the celebrations, were soon surrounded by people dancing and chant-ing. A small harp of African design, decorated with shells and charms was being plucked by a musician. Also of African origin was the skirt of goats' hooves worn by one of the dancers; it produced a rattling sound, rather like maracas. To the beat of a single hand-drum and the occa-sional blast of a horn, tribesmen from Oman started an impromptu dance with rifles and daggers, developing into an agile sword dance. Away from the crowd, a group of women tripped back and forth, trailing scarves of light chiffon in the breeze. Another group, shy at such a large gathering, began to dance farther away on the sands. A dignified tribal dance was also being performed, the men moving in uni-son, holding their rifles above them and, from time to time, calling out the name of their tribe. Occasionally, when they were joined by one of

**Page 154 and 155** Apart from the main occasions for public celebrations – religious holidays, weddings and circumcisions – dancing would occur spontaneously to celebrate good news. These tribesmen on the sands of Qoran at Ras al Khaima had just heard that there was to be a feast. **Left and above** A flag is hoisted to mark the site for the start of a celebration.

their Shaikhs, they fired the guns, one-handed, above their heads.

As the sun sank, most people made their way home for the evening prayers. The music and dancing were halted so that those who remained could pray on the spot. Hurricane lamps were suspended from flag-poles, and a small number, perhaps sailors or visiting tribesmen, continued the celebration when the town was in darkness. The drums boomed at a different pitch now, as the high humidity created a mist and the drumskins slackened. The celebrations would be resumed the next day, until the event had been suitably honoured.

**Above** A sword-dancer disproves gravity.
**Below** Ancient swords and a drum – and a
sandal making do as a shield are all that's
needed for this impromptu celebration. **Right**
A skirt of goats' hooves provides this group of
music-makers with a rhythmic rattling like
maracas.

**Above** The musical instruments for public celebrations were of varied origin – the harp with its skin-clad sound box came of African provenance, for example, as well as the charms dangling from it. **Right** The goat-hide drum was universal.

This shawm-like instrument was of Baluchi origin.

Summoned by the throb of the drum, people emerged from town or village, to mingle and lose themselves among the groups of dancers – the dignified tribesmen swaying to the chant of their tribe's name and firing their rifles into the air, the leaping sword dancers, and many another drum-driven group. **Below** Set apart from the main festivities, this group of ladies are engaged in their own traditional dance, the *noban*.

# YOUNG ARABIANS

ALTHOUGH children inevitably suffered the same austerity and hardship as their parents, they also shared the joys and festivities. Boys – except the very young, who were left in the care of their mothers – were introduced early to the ways of adulthood. They would accompany their fathers, watching over the camels and goats, tending the palm trees, netting and drying fish, or sitting in a market booth. They soon acquired skills and the lore of desert or sea. They would sit among grown-ups, learning from the talk, just as the sons of Shaikhs would frequently sit alongside their fathers in open *majlis*, acquiring the art of adjudication. When they first displayed signs of maturity, their fathers were congratulated. The boy had 'arrived'.

With no record of births or keeping of birthdays, few people knew their precise age. At best, the time of their birth might be linked to some notable event – 'the year of heavy rainfall' or the year one tribe fought another. My photographs, accompanied by dates in my diaries, have been a pleasant surprise to some, less pleasing to others.

Illiteracy does not mean ignorance. Many of these people were masters of the spoken word and some were poets; a discerning audience would listen, absorbed, to their narrations. Putting words on paper was a skill for which they had no need; but illiterate fathers were keen for their sons to acquire it for anyone who could read the Koran was highly regarded. Children of the ruling Shaikhs were placed for this purpose under the tutelage of a *Mattawa*. The teacher having been paid for his services, other children were allowed to attend the lessons; such small classes were held wherever a teacher was available – in mosques or in a spare room, in a *barasti* hut on the shore or beneath a palm. For the sons of merchants, arithmetic was added, enabling them to keep accounts.

On several occasions I was enchanted to watch the graduation of girls from a Koran class. It was a moment of great pride for them and the teacher. Wearing new, brightly coloured, dresses, the graduates were laden with gold jewellery, usually belonging to their mothers or lent by well-wishers. As this pretty little group, accompanied by their teacher, moved through the town, each of the graduates would sing a verse from the Koran, followed at the end of every sentence by the chorus of her classmates crying 'Amen', from which the ceremony took its name – *Tawmina*. In the market and at the houses of prominent families, the teacher would receive small gifts of money as an acknowledgement of his good work.

If toys were lacking, play was not. A swimming race, sliding headfirst down a steep sand dune, painting on dry sand with a muddy mixture from the well, a game of 'Dhabb' based on the outline of a lizard pressed into the sand – these were fun. And there were simply made, skilfully sailed boats. But who needed toys when one could go hunting with one's father?

In some ways, no doubt, the quality of life may sometimes have been better before the coming of today's material benefits, but I have one vivid memory to redress the balance. It is of a bright-eyed young boy, snuggled into his father for comfort, as we sat around the coffee pot in a distant settlement of Liwa. He was very ill from an enormous, ugly growth on his head, too ill for a lengthy journey by camel. I promised to take him with me when I called back at the settlement in two or three days' time. But when I returned, the light in those young eyes had been extinguished and he lay beneath the sand.

**Previous page** These boys demonstrate their instinct for seafaring by the skill with which they made and sail their model boats. A camel stick is used for a mast, the hull is fashioned from a petrol tin and a sail from a loin cloth. **Right** A young Shaikh – one of the sons of the Ruler of Ajman – takes part in a swimming race down a sand dune.

**Above** Decked in their finery for *Eid al Fitr* one girl shows her friend the model of his boat made by her father on a recent journey to East Africa. **Right** In their best clothes and bedizened in gold, these girls tour the town after graduating from their Koran class, each singing a verse from the Koran, followed by a chorussed 'Amen' from her classmates.

In an open-sided *barasti* hut on the shore at Fujairah, boys rock back and forth as they read to their teacher from the Koran.

Two young Shaikhs of Abu Dhabi. Boyish,
but displaying signs of maturity which greatly
pleased their fathers with whom they would
sit in *majlis* acquiring the skills of leadership,
mediation and diplomacy.

# _ENVOI_
# NEWS OF THE WORLD AT REST

THE ARRIVAL of any traveller was a major event. Everyone would rise for a dignified exchange of greetings. 'Peace be on you' the newcomer would exclaim, making a slow sweeping gesture round the assembled company with the open palm of his outstretched right hand. 'And on you be peace' would come the rejoinder.

This age-old exchange was followed by a physical greeting, the form of which depended on the relationship between those involved. Sometimes it was the touching of the fingers of the right hand, which were held in contact during the salutations but without the pumping action of a Western handshake. Or it took the form of a 'nose kiss', three brushing movements of the nose, left to right, right to left and a centre press. Then followed solemn enquiries after each others' health, rejoinders praising and thanking the Almighty, and a repetition of the same questions when seated, each looking earnestly into the other's eyes as though to find the answer. As with the English 'how do you do?', factual replies were not really expected in this early stage of the proceedings.

After a polite interval the traveller would be asked the critical question, 'What is the news?', to which the standard reply was 'None – the world is resting.' The same question and answer might be exchanged several times during these unhurried preliminaries. The apparent nonchalance and self-control of a traveller who was inwardly bursting to tell his news were a delight to behold. His material possessions might be few, his rifle and dagger unremarkable, his only shirt old and grubby: but he had news. He would give it only when every face was turned towards him. It was his prize possession which he must be coaxed into surrendering and would eventually deliver with a strong sense of stage-craft.

Without newspapers, radios or telephones, quite nearby places seemed remote. News was transmitted from mouth to mouth, inevitably with embellishments and distortions. The more dramatic items would survive to become sagas or at least good yarns, passed on for the younger generations to savour. But memories grow dim, and much is lost.